COLORS of HOPE

An Inspirational Coloring Book

LISA JOY SAMSON

Revell

a division of Baker Publishing Group
Grand Rapids, Michigan

© 2017 by Lisa Joy Samson

Published by Revell
a division of Baker Publishing Group
P.O. Box 6287, Grand Rapids, MI 49516-6287
www.revellbooks.com

Printed in the United States of America

ISBN 978-0-8007-2831-1

17 18 19 20 21 22 23   7 6 5 4 3 2 1

This book is dedicated
to my three children plus one.
Ty,
Jake,
McLeod,
and Matt.
You four give me hope
for the future of this world.
I love you all.

An INVITATION from LISA JOY

I'm so excited, aren't you? A fresh new collection of pictures to color! How much do we love that new book smell? And a coloring book? Even better! Let's go for a ride together! I'll bring the outlines, you bring your favorite markers, crayons, colored pencils, and gel pens for an adventure of artistic expression.

There are so many designs ready for you to add your bright, artful touch. Butterflies, trees, flowers, bees, and stained glass designs, all hand drawn for a look that says, "There's real art going on here, everybody!"

Not only that, tucked inside like hidden treasure (what adventure is complete without that?) are time-honored Bible verses, carefully chosen to help keep hope alive in your life. God is, and he is able to do abundantly above all that we could ask for, or even think! Isn't that the best news?

There are so many benefits to this book, from just plain having fun and expressing your creativity, to the mental health benefits coloring provides through the use of small motor skills. As well, *Colors of Hope* designs are suitable for framing and come in groups of four for wall arrangements. You deserve to show off your work. (Hint: How special would it be to offer your artwork as presents to your loved ones? I know I would love receiving such a personal and loving gift.)

Enjoy! May love and hope color your world at the dawning of each new day. And pretty please, feel free to post your finished designs at our Facebook page, Lisa Joy Samson.

Much love,

Lisa Joy

ACKNOWLEDGMENTS

Thanks be to God, the world, including friends and family, and all who support the work of artists everywhere. Particularly, I'd like to express gratitude to my agent, Chip MacGregor, who shopped a coloring book and blazed new territory for me. To Vicki Crumpton at Revell, who took a chance and championed the work, I am thankful beyond measure. God bless you both. I would also like to thank all of my readers who have traveled with me from the literary realm to the realm of lines and colors. God bless you too! And thank you, God, for the care you give your children, particularly this one. My hope is in you.

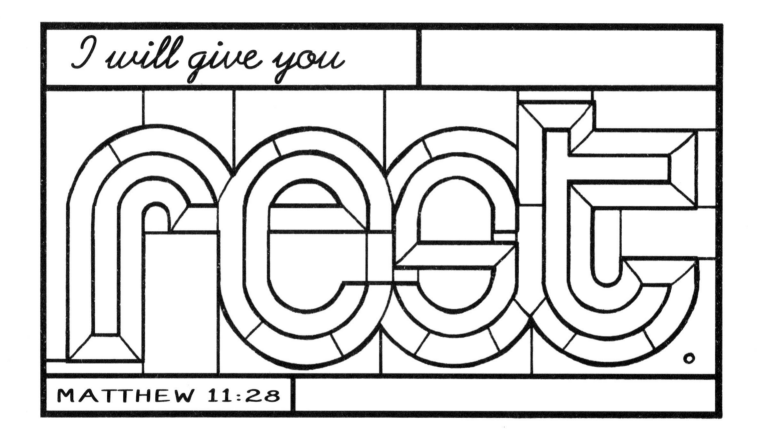

I will give you rest

MATTHEW 11:28

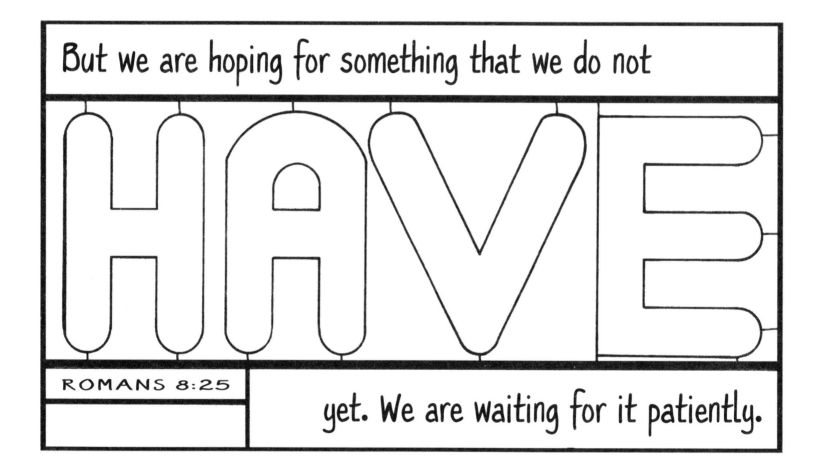

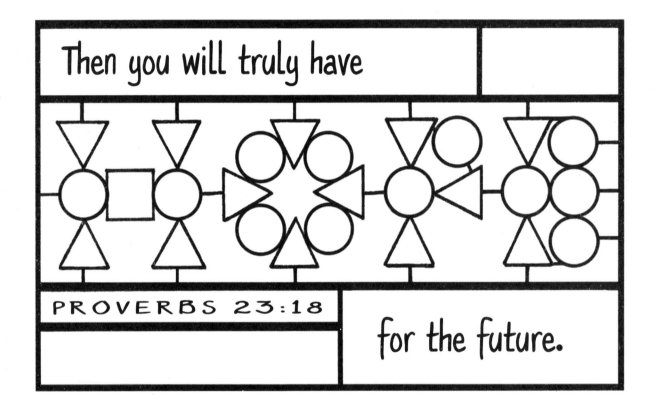

Then you will truly have

PROVERBS 23:18

for the future.

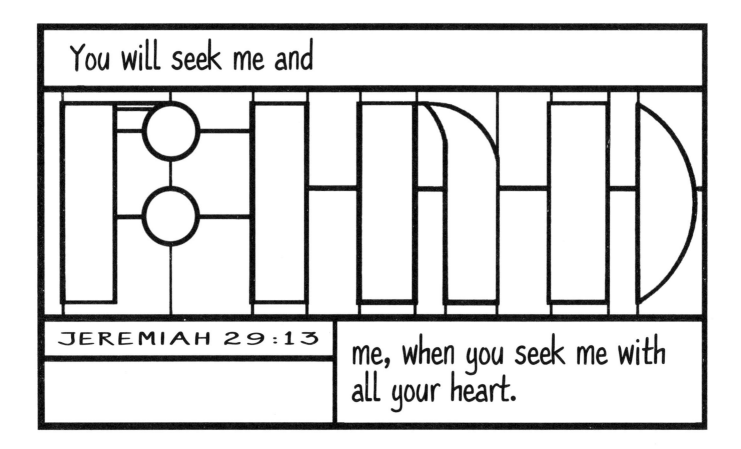

I pray that your hearts will be flooded with light so that you can understand the confident

hope

EPHESIANS 1:18

he has given to those he called.

Hope

I wait for the Lord, my soul waits, and in his word I

PSALM 130:5

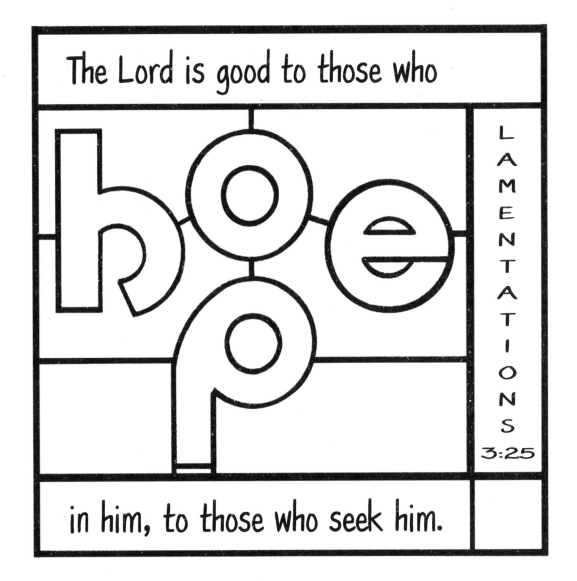

The Lord is good to those who

hope

in him, to those who seek him.

LAMENTATIONS 3:25

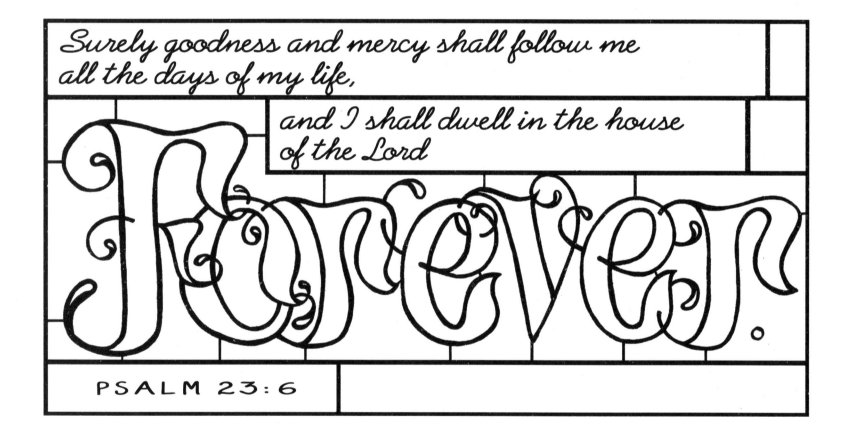

Surely goodness and mercy shall follow me all the days of my life, and I shall dwell in the house of the Lord Forever.

PSALM 23:6

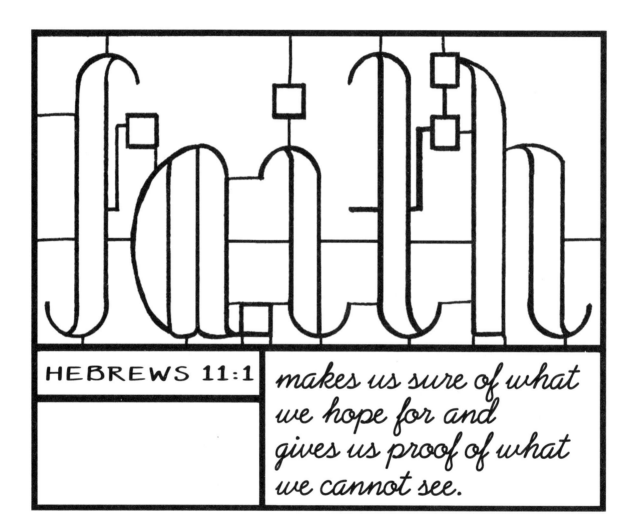

HEBREWS 11:1 *makes us sure of what we hope for and gives us proof of what we cannot see.*

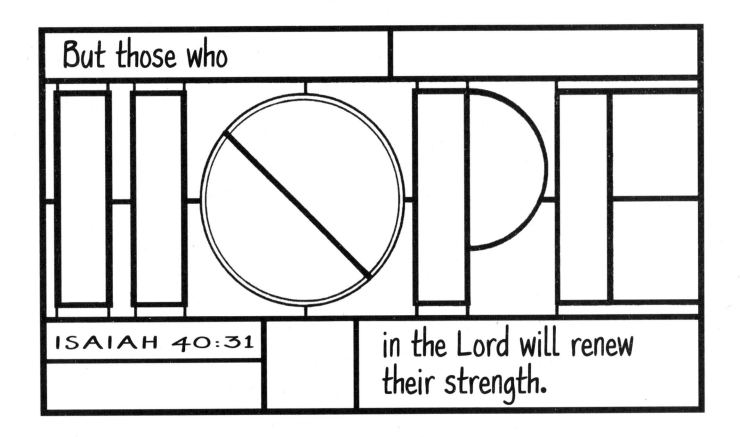

But those who HOPE in the Lord will renew their strength.

ISAIAH 40:31

I will always put my hope in you;
I will

PRAISE

PSALM 71:14

you more and more.

Be strong in heart,
all you who

PSALM 31:24

in the Lord.

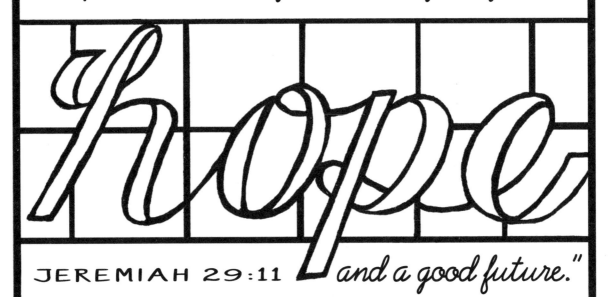

"I know what I am planning for you," says the Lord. "I have good plans for you, not plans to hurt you. I will give you *hope* and a good future."

JEREMIAH 29:11

When you call out to me and

Come

JEREMIAH 29:12

and pray to me,
I'll hear you.

For we through the Spirit, by

GALATIANS 5:5

are waiting for the hope of righteousness.

Overflow with **hope** by the power of the Holy Spirit.

ROMANS 15:13

This is why we work hard and continue to struggle, for our hope is in the living God, who is the Savior of

1 TIMOTHY 4:10

people.

No one who waits for you will ever

BIBLE

PSALM 25:3 put to shame.

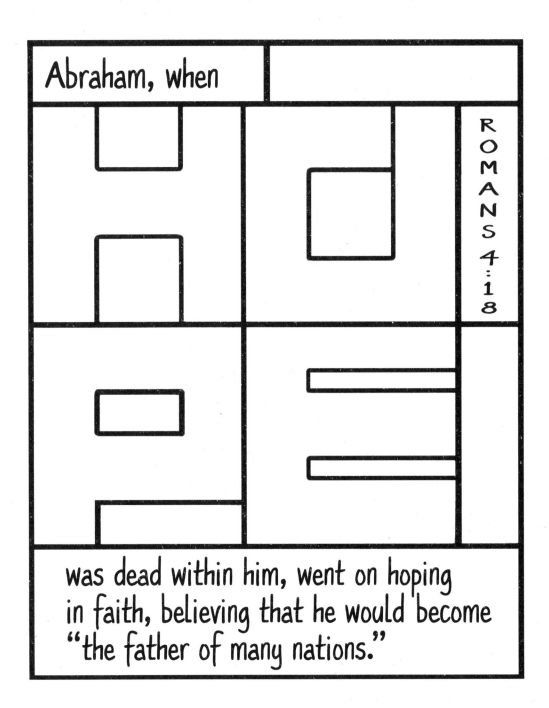

Abraham, when

ROMANS 4:18

was dead within him, went on hoping
in faith, believing that he would become
"the father of many nations."

Even when I walk through a valley of deep darkness, I will not be afraid because you are with me. Your rod and your staff—they

PSALM 23:4

me.

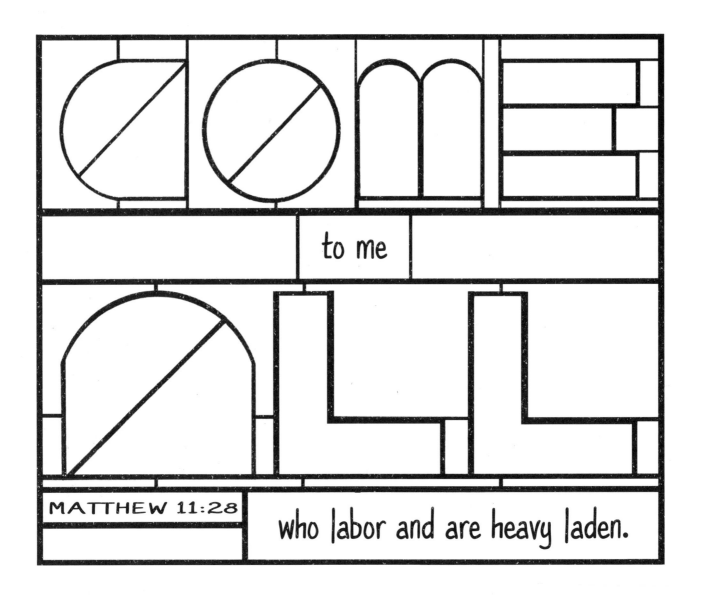

COME to me ALL

MATTHEW 11:28

who labor and are heavy laden.

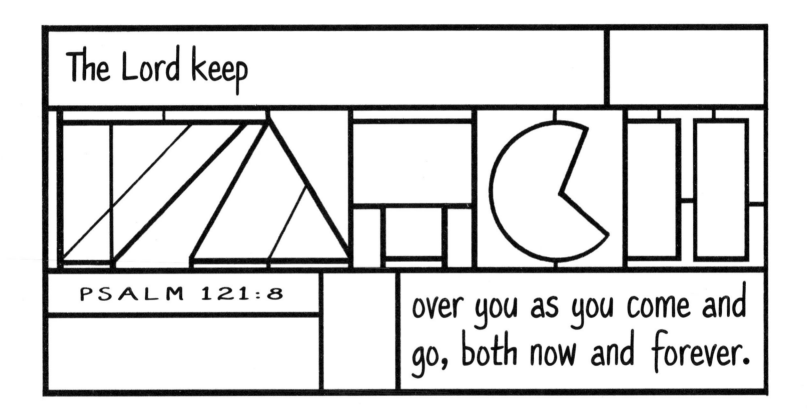

The Lord keep

PSALM 121:8

over you as you come and go, both now and forever.

God did not send his Son into the world to judge the world guilty, but to save the

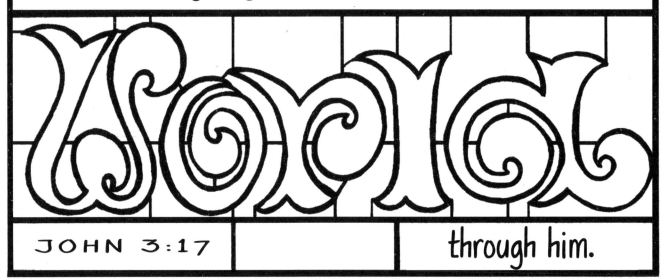

JOHN 3:17

through him.

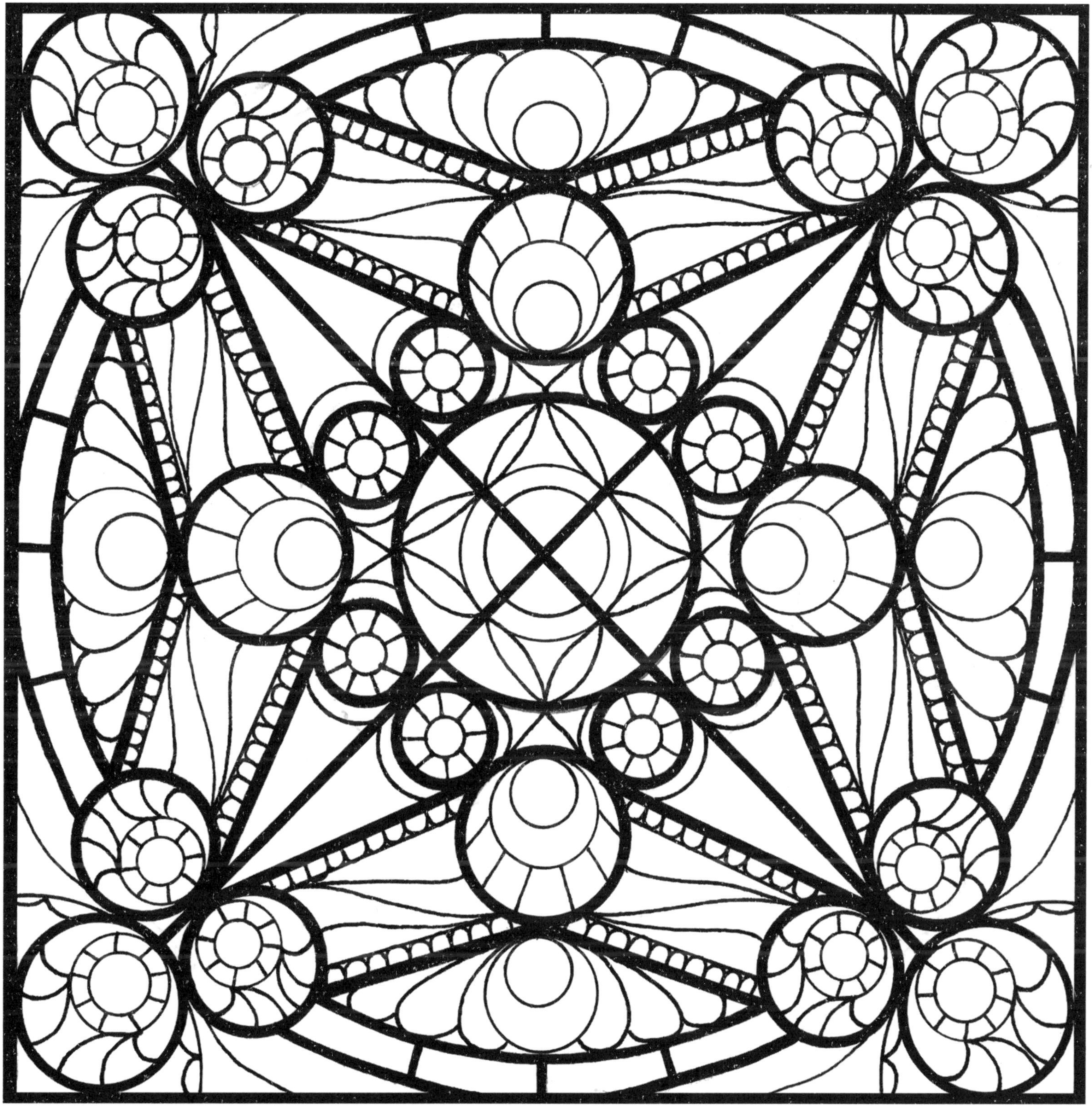

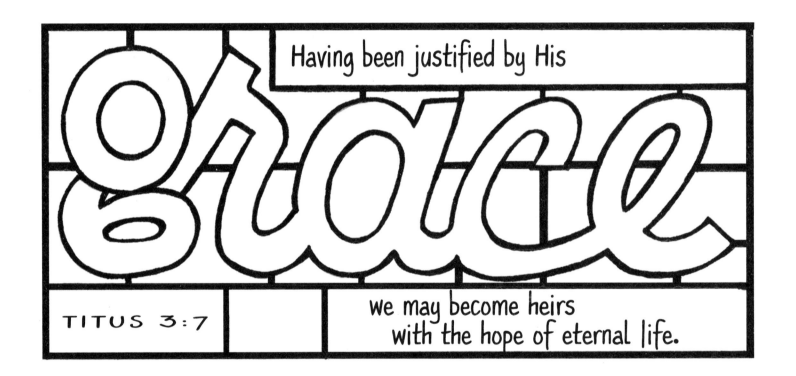

Having been justified by His

grace

TITUS 3:7

we may become heirs
with the hope of eternal life.

Lead me by your **TRUTH** and teach me, for you are the God who saves me. All day long I put my hope in you.

PSALM 25:5

By awesome deeds you answer us with deliverance, O God of our salvation; you are the

hope

PSALM 65:5

of all the ends of the earth and of the farthest seas.

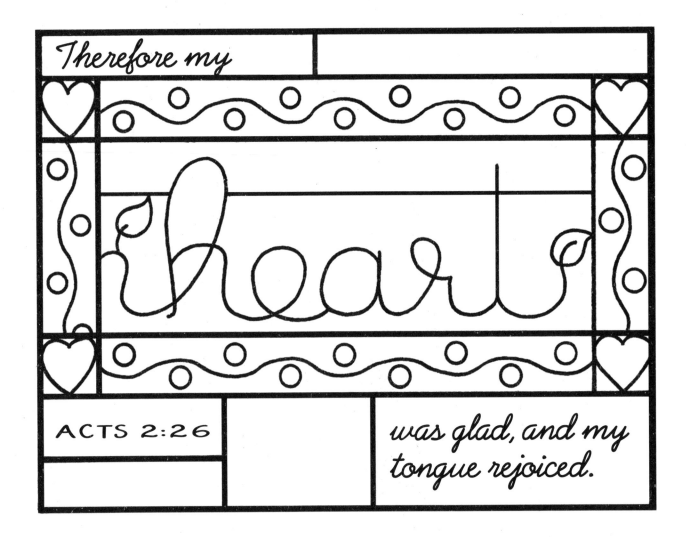

Therefore my **heart** was glad, and my tongue rejoiced.

ACTS 2:26

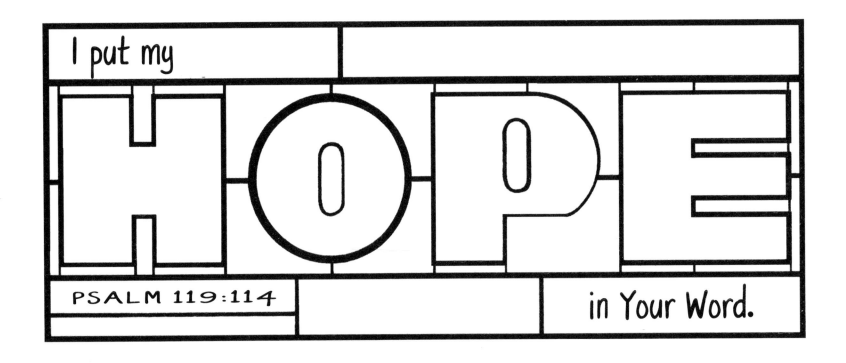

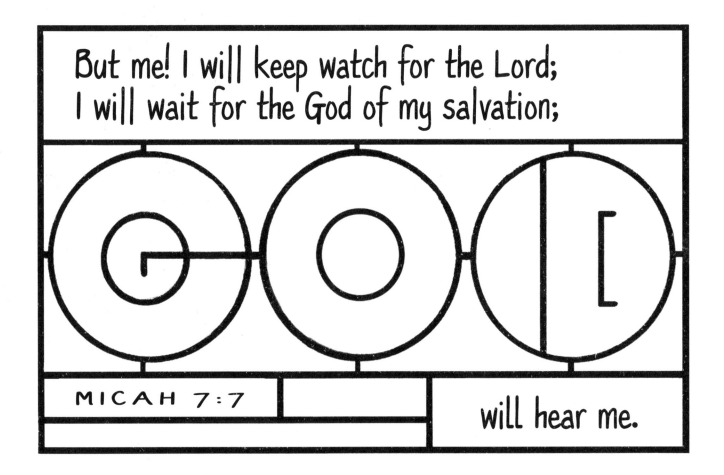

But me! I will keep watch for the Lord;
I will wait for the God of my salvation;

MICAH 7:7

will hear me.

Let us hold on firmly to the **HOPE** we profess, because we can trust God to keep his promise.

HEBREWS 10:23

Lord, may your gracious LOVE be upon us, even as we hope in you.

PSALM 33:22

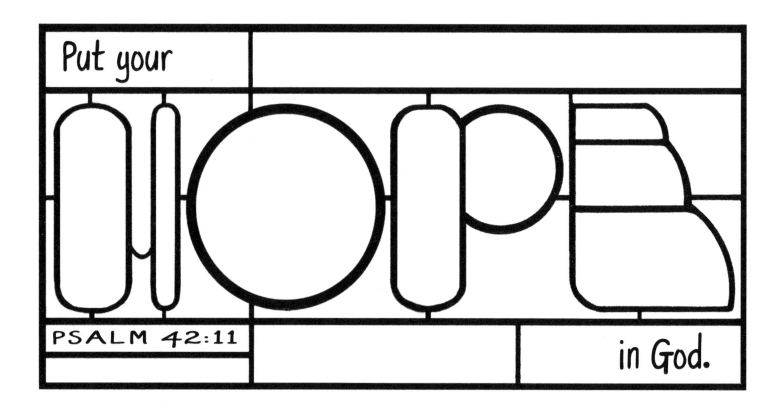

Put your **HOPE** in God.

PSALM 42:11

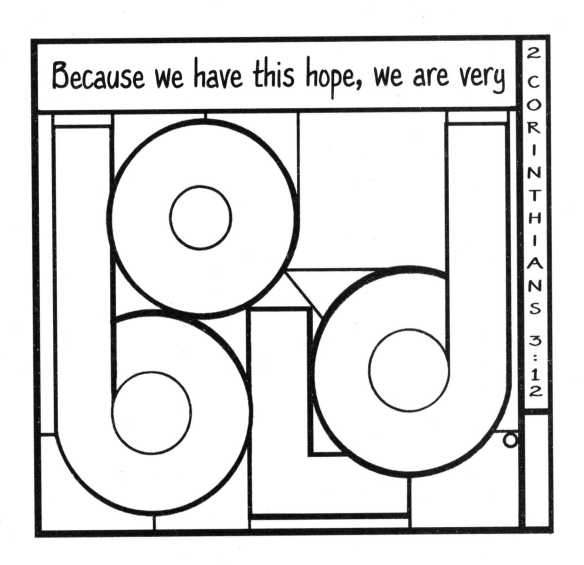

Because we have this hope, we are very BOLD

2 CORINTHIANS 3:12

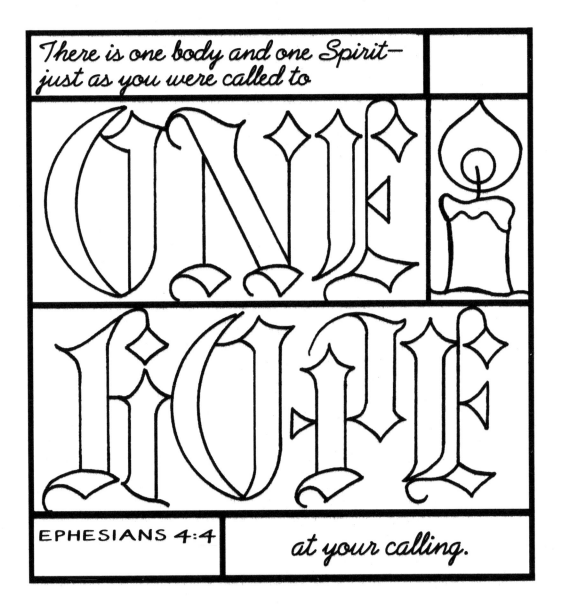

There is one body and one Spirit—
just as you were called to

ONE

HOPE

EPHESIANS 4:4

at your calling.

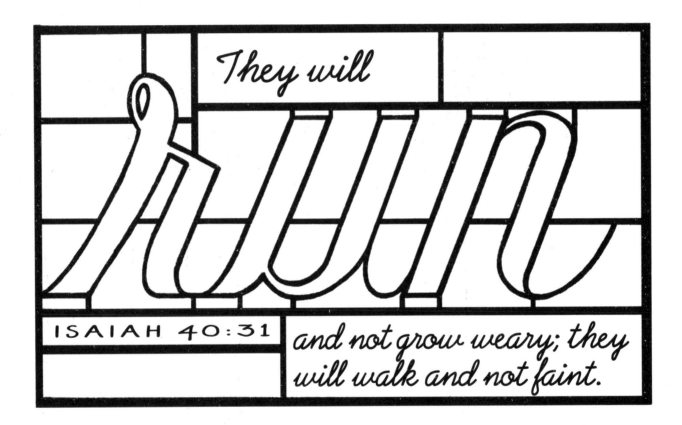

They will **RUN**

ISAIAH 40:31

and not grow weary; they will walk and not faint.

There is one body and one Spirit—
just as you were called to

ONE

EPHESIANS 4:4   hope at your calling.

The LORD is my shepherd, I shall not want. He makes me lie down in green pastures; he leads me beside still waters; he restores my

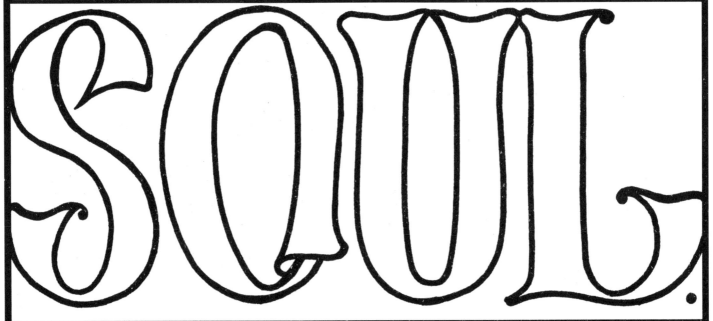

SOUL.

PSALM 23:1—3

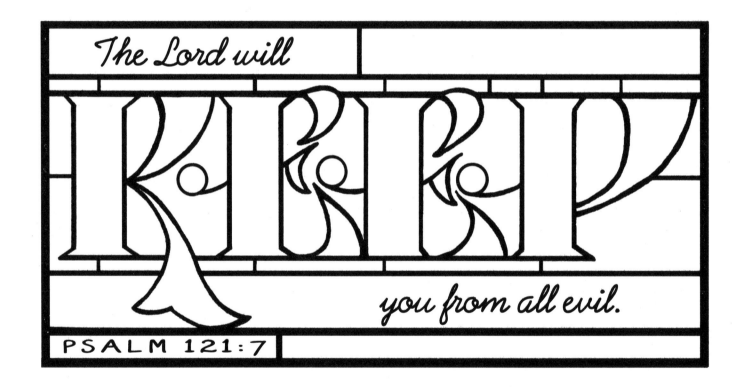

Hope does not disappoint us, because God's

ROMANS 5:5

has been poured into our hearts through the Holy Spirit that has been given to us.

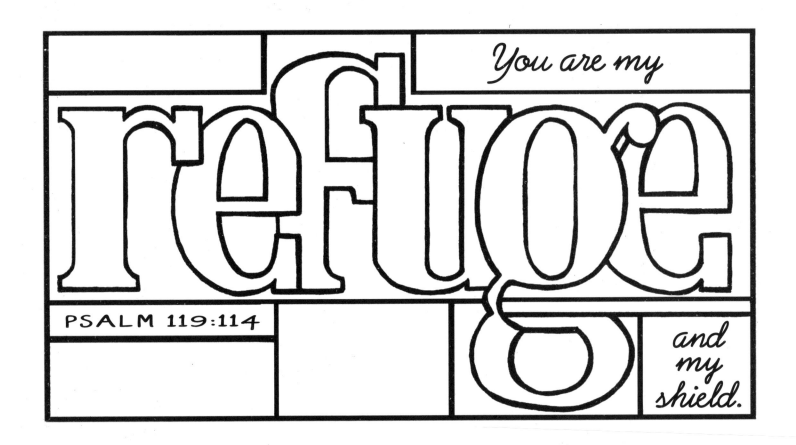

You are my refuge and my shield.

PSALM 119:114

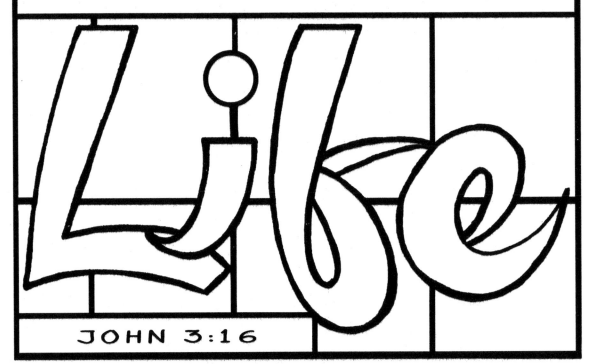

For God loved the world so much that he gave his only Son, so that everyone who believes in him may not die but have eternal

Life

JOHN 3:16

May God, the source of hope, fill you with JOY and PEACE ROMANS 15:13 through your faith in him.

Lisa Joy Samson is the author of nearly forty books, including *Quaker Summer*, which was named novel of the year by both Women of Faith and *Christianity Today*. Her chief creative love has always been art, and she has designed book covers, invitations, and artful signage. Hailing from Baltimore, Maryland, she currently lives in Colorado Springs, Colorado, with her daughter.